Funster 600+ Funniest Dad Jokes Book

Charles Timmerman
Founder of Funster.com

This book includes free Sudoku and word search
puzzles that are available here:

funster.com/bonus30

You can also join the *Funster VIP Newsletter* and be
the first to find out about our new books.

ISBN: 978-1-953561-07-7

A Special Request

Your brief Amazon review could <u>really</u> help us. This link will take you to the Amazon.com review page for this book:

funster.com/review30

Dear Reader,

Dads will do almost anything for a laugh. And for us dads, a groan is good enough. With this goal in mind, dad jokes were born.

My love of dad jokes began when my dad referred to the bathroom as the bat-room right after we watched *Batman* on TV. I thought it was hilarious, and he used that joke for the next 40 years. If only Dad had this book to give him some fresh material!

Nowadays, I text dad jokes to my older daughters. Most of the time, I'm rewarded with the laughing emoji in reply. It makes me feel good. But who am I kidding? I know there isn't a groaning emoji. 😆

This book is filled with the funniest family-friendly dad jokes I could find. They're good for everyone, not just dads. Pick out your favorites and share them with the people in your life. They'll love them!

Charles Timmmm

To be Frank, I'd have to change my name. 😆

The invention of the wheel was what got things rolling.

What do you call an indecisive bee? A may-bee.

I saw a thousand-year-old oil stain. It was from ancient Greece.

Did you hear the one about the guy with the broken hearing aid? Neither did he.

Justice is a dish best served cold. If it were served warm, it would be justwater.

I only seem to get sick on weekdays. I must have a weekend immune system.

Broken guitar for sale. No strings attached.

What is the opposite of a croissant? A happy uncle.

Not to brag, but I made six figures last year. I was also named worst employee at the toy factory.

What on the playground is always exhausted? The tire swing.

What has to be broken before you can use it? An egg!

What's the best time to go to the dentist? Tooth-hurty.

What do you get when you divide the circumference of a jack-o-lantern by its diameter? Pumpkin Pi!

What's the difference between a pickpocket and an umpire? One steals watches and one watches steals.

My wife asked me to go get 6 cans of Sprite from the grocery store. I realized when I got home that I had picked 7 up.

Man, I love my furniture. Me and my recliner go way back.

I went to the zoo and saw a piece of toast in a cage. The sign said, "bread in captivity".

What do you call a fish with two knees? A two-knee fish!

I'll tell you what often gets overlooked: garden fences.

What gets wetter the more it dries? A towel.

Of all the inventions of the last 100 years, the whiteboard has to be the most remarkable.

Have you seen a car with zero tires? It is totally unwheel.

I quit the art class. It was a little too sketchy.

If it weren't for Venetian blinds, it would be curtains for everybody.

If I ever find the doctor
who screwed up my limb
replacement surgery, I'll kill him
with my bear hands!

Why can't Cinderella play
soccer? Because she's always
running away from the ball.

Someone told me that I should
write a book. I said, "That's a
novel concept."

I have kleptomania, but when it
gets bad, I take something for it.

No matter how much you
push the envelope, it'll still be
stationery.

I couldn't figure out how the
seat belt worked. Then it just
clicked.

Why was the baby in Egypt? It was looking for its mummy.

Why do fathers take an extra pair of socks when they go golfing? In case they get a hole in one!

What's another name for a clever duck? Wise quacker!

Did you hear about the kidnapping at school? It's okay; he woke up.

Where do bees go to the bathroom? At the BP station.

A couple of yogurt cups walk into a country club and the bartender says, "We don't serve your kind here." "Why not?" one yogurt cup asks. "We're cultured."

Why is the thing you're searching for always in the last place you look? Because when you find it, you stop looking.

Why did the student eat his homework? Because his teacher told him it would be a piece of cake!

A bear walks into a restaurant and says, "I want a grilled... cheese." The waiter asks, "Why the big pause?" The bear replies, "I don't know. I was born with them."

What is the leading cause of dry skin? Towels.

What type of medicine do ants use when they have eye problems? Ant-eye-biotics.

What do you call a man named David without an ID? Dav.

Doctor: "I think your DNA is backwards." Me: "AND?"

I was going to get a brain transplant, but I changed my mind.

Our wedding was so beautiful, even the cake was in tiers.

What do you get when the post office burns down? A case of black mail.

I wondered why the Frisbee kept getting bigger and bigger. Then it hit me.

My landlord told me we need to talk about the heating bill. "Sure," I said. "My door is always open."

A panic-stricken man said to his doctor, "You have to help me! I think I'm shrinking!" "Now settle down," the doctor calmly told him. "You'll just have to learn to be a little patient."

What's green and fuzzy and will kill you if it falls from a tree? A pool table!

Why do bees hum? Because they don't know the words.

What do you call a sad berry? A blueberry.

Did you know that milk is the fastest liquid on earth? It's pasteurized before you can even see it.

What do you get when a turkey lays an egg on top of a barn? An egg roll.

I have a joke about a broken clock, but it's not the right time.

Why was the big cat disqualified from the race? Because it was a cheetah.

Why did the pencil cross the road? It was lead!

I was in a grocery store when a man started to throw cheese, butter, and yogurt at me. How dairy!

Why didn't the skeleton go to the dance? Because he had no body to go with.

Parallel lines have so much in common. It's a shame they'll never meet.

Why is it pointless to tell a cow a joke? They've probably herd it before.

Did you hear about the guy whose whole left side was cut off? He's all right now.

What did the grape do when he got stepped on? He let out a little wine.

Linda broke her finger today. On the other hand, she was completely fine.

If you think swimming with dolphins is expensive, you should try swimming with sharks. It cost me an arm and a leg!

Why is it so hard for a cucumber to become a pickle? It's a jarring process!

Why are peppers the best at archery? Because they habanero!

The best gift I ever received was a broken drum. You can't beat that.

I saw an ad in a shop window: "Television for sale, $1, volume stuck on full." I thought, I can't turn that down.

Why do we tell actors to "break a leg"? Because every play has a cast.

How does the moon cut its hair? Eclipse it.

I went to the butcher's the other day and bet him $50 that he couldn't reach the meat on the top shelf. "No," he said, "the steaks are too high."

What did the digital clock say to the grandfather clock? "Look, no hands!"

Don't trust that big cat. He's lion.

Why did the burglar hang his mug shot on the wall? To prove that he was framed!

Which state has the most streets? Rhode Island.

I got an email the other day teaching me how to read maps backwards. Turns out it was just spam.

How are opera singers and sailors alike? They both have to handle the high C's!

How do you get a blind person to see? Usually by boat.

My dog is a genius. I asked him, "What's two minus two?" He said nothing.

What is a witch's favorite subject in school? Spelling.

Why was the baby ant confused? Because all his uncles were ants.

My writer friend claims he glued himself to his autobiography. I don't believe him, but that's his story and he's sticking to it.

I had a fun childhood. My dad used to push me down the hill in old tires. They were Goodyears.

Americans can't switch from pounds to kilograms overnight. That would cause mass confusion.

I'm practicing for a bug-eating contest, and I've got butterflies in my stomach.

My new sweater had a problem with static, so I returned it. They gave me a new one free of charge.

Why did the triangle feel sorry for the circle? Because it's pointless!

Why do tigers have stripes? So they don't get spotted!

I only know 25 letters of the alphabet. I don't know Y.

Why do trees look suspicious on sunny days? They just seem a little shady!

I tried to win a sun-tanning competition. But all I got was bronze.

Can February March? No, but April May.

What do you call a cow that won't give milk? A Milk Dud.

What country's capital is growing the fastest? Ireland. Every day it's Dublin.

I cut my finger shredding cheese, but I think that I may have grater problems.

Why does the baker go to work?
Because he kneads the dough.

The new mechanic lost his job;
they say he lacks fine motor
skills.

Every day I tell my wife I'm
going to jog around the
neighborhood, but I never do.
It's a running joke I have.

I fear for the calendar; its days
are numbered.

A guy walks into a bar. And
that's how he lost the limbo
contest.

To whoever stole my copy of
Microsoft Office, I will find you.
You have my Word.

For Valentine's Day, I decided to get my wife some beads for an abacus. It's the little things that count.

I could never be a plumber. It's too hard watching your life's work go down the drain.

What did the tie say to the hat? "You go on ahead. I'll hang around."

Want to hear a joke about going to the bathroom? Urine for a treat.

Why are piggy banks so wise? They're filled with common cents.

The Lego shop reopens tomorrow, but I recommend avoiding it for now. People will be lined up for blocks.

Why was the robot so tired after his road trip? He had a hard drive.

What did Marie say about her brain surgeon? "I really gave him a piece of my mind!"

What room does a ghost not need? A living room.

My boss told me to have a good day, so I went home.

Why did the crab never share? Because he's shellfish.

What do you call two monkeys who share an Amazon account? Prime mates.

How do you fix a cracked pumpkin? A pumpkin patch.

Why was Santa's tiny helper feeling depressed? Because he had low elf-esteem.

My boss told me to attach two pieces of wood together. I totally nailed it!

I wanted to go on a diet, but I feel like I have way too much on my plate right now.

What stays in the corner yet can travel all over the world? A postage stamp.

My kid wants to invent a pencil with an eraser on each end, but I just don't see the point.

The difference between a numerator and a denominator is a short line. Only a fraction of people will understand this.

Why was the mushroom the life of the party? It was a fungi.

What do you call a cow with a twitch? Beef jerky!

I tried to start a professional hide-and-seek team, but it didn't work out. Turns out, good players are hard to find.

So what if I don't know what apocalypse means? It's not the end of the world.

Why did the dinosaur cross the road? Because chickens hadn't evolved yet!

What should you do if someone rolls their eyes at you? Roll them back!

What's the difference between a guitar and a fish? You can tune a guitar, but you can't tuna fish!

The shovel was a ground-breaking invention.

Every time I take my dog to the park, the ducks try to bite him. That's what I get for buying a pure-bread dog.

I used to think I was indecisive, but now I'm not sure.

Which is faster, hot or cold? Hot, because you can catch a cold.

A weasel walks into a bar. The bartender says, "Wow, I've never served a weasel before. What can I get for you?" "Pop," goes the weasel.

Why couldn't the astronaut book a hotel on the moon? Because it was full.

What did one eye say to the other? Between you and me, something smells.

There's a new type of broom out; it's sweeping the nation.

Why do melons have weddings? Because they cantaloupe.

I was just reminiscing about the beautiful herb garden I had when I was growing up. Good thymes.

Why did Mozart sell his chickens? They kept saying, "Bach, Bach, Bach."

Why can't you ever run through a campsite? You can only ran – it's always past tents.

How do you fix a broken tomato? With a can of tomato paste.

Did you hear about the eyeglasses maker who moved his shop to an island off Alaska and is now known as an optical Aleutian?

Two goldfish are in a tank. One says to the other, "Do you know how to drive this thing?"

How do you deal with a fear of speed bumps? You slowly get over it.

How many apples grow on a tree? All of them.

I gave all my dead batteries away today, free of charge.

Sometimes I tuck my knees into my chest and lean forward. That's just how I roll.

Why can't your hand be 12 inches long? Because then it would be a foot.

A book just fell on my head. I only have my shelf to blame.

What do you need to make a small fortune on Wall Street? A large fortune.

The best time on a clock is 6:30 – hands down.

How do you make a waterbed bouncier? Add spring water.

What do you get from a pampered cow? Spoiled milk.

Plateaus are the highest form of flattery.

How can you tell when a bucket gets sick? It becomes a little pale.

What do you call a hippie's wife? Mississippi.

What happened to the man who sued an airline for losing his luggage? He lost his case!

The rotation of Earth really makes my day.

What do you call a shoe made from a banana? A slipper.

Why does Norway have barcodes on their battleships? So when they get back to port, they can Scandinavian.

Why did the boy tiptoe past the medicine cabinet? He didn't want to wake up the sleeping pills!

Why couldn't the pirate play cards? Because he was sitting on the deck!

You know, people pick their nose, but I just feel like I was born with mine.

My mouth has turned into a flower bed. It has tulips.

What falls in winter but never gets hurt? Snow.

I'm on a seafood diet. I see food and I eat it.

I burnt my Hawaiian pizza today. I should have set the oven to aloha temperature.

My doctor told me I'm going deaf. The news was hard for me to hear.

We're renovating the house, and the first floor is going great, but the second floor is another story.

Chances are if you've seen one shopping center, you've seen a mall.

How many ears did Davy Crockett have? His right ear, his left ear, and his wild front-ear.

I'm reading a horror story in Braille. Something bad is going to happen. I can just feel it.

I had a rough day, and then somebody went and ripped the front and back pages out of my dictionary. It just goes from bad to worse.

If April showers bring May flowers, what do May flowers bring? Pilgrims.

What did one snowman say to another? Do you smell carrots?

I wish I could clean mirrors for a living. It's just something I can see myself doing.

Why do pirates not know the alphabet? They always get stuck at "C".

Did you get a haircut? No, I got them all cut.

When do doctors get angry?
When they run out of patients.

What is more peculiar than
watching a catfish? Watching a
goldfish bowl.

What do you call cattle with
a sense of humor? Laughing
stock.

Somebody stole all my lamps. I
couldn't be more de-lighted!

What do dentists call their
x-rays? Tooth pics!

I hated facial hair, but then it
grew on me.

What is an astronaut's favorite
key on a computer keyboard?
The space bar.

If at first you don't succeed, skydiving is not for you!

Why couldn't the bicycle stand up by itself? It was two-tired.

An invisible man married an invisible woman. The kids were nothing to look at either.

Why did the invisible man turn down the job offer? He couldn't see himself doing it.

What do you call a sleeping bull? A bulldozer.

Why are spiders so smart? They can find everything on the web.

What happens when a strawberry gets run over crossing the street? Traffic jam.

Why did the girl smear peanut butter on the road? To go with the traffic jam.

What has more letters than the alphabet? The post office!

My therapist told me I have problems expressing my emotions. Can't say I'm surprised.

What has one head, one foot, and four legs? A bed.

I spent a lot of time, money, and effort childproofing my house... but the kids still get in.

What did the limestone say to the geologist? Don't take me for granite.

Never date a tennis player. Love means nothing to them.

My dad was born a conjoined twin but separated at birth. So I have an uncle, once removed.

How do you cut the sea in half? With a seesaw!

As a scarecrow, people say I'm outstanding in my field. But hay, it's in my jeans.

Did you hear about the square that got into a car accident? Yeah, now he's a rect-angle!

How do you throw a party in outer space? You planet.

Why are elevator jokes so good? Because they work on so many levels.

What's the easiest way to burn 1,000 calories? Leave the pizza in the oven.

What do you call an ant that has been shunned by his community? A socially-dissed ant.

How can you tell a vampire has a cold? They start coffin.

Do you know where you can get chicken broth in bulk? The stock market.

Did you know that crocodiles can grow up to 15 feet? But most only have four.

I want to go on record that I support farming. In fact, you could call me protractor.

Why did the bullet end up losing his job? He got fired.

What did the bald man say when he received a comb for a present? "Thanks, I'll never part with it."

Swords will never become obsolete. They're cutting-edge technology.

Why was the student's report card wet? It was below "C" level!

Teacher: "John, where are the Great Plains?" John: "At the airport."

Why is it hard to understand volunteers? Because they make no cents.

What's the worst Dad joke ever? This one!

I'm attaching a light to the ceiling, but I'm afraid I'll screw it up.

Why should you never tell a pig your secret? Because it is sure to squeal.

I knew I shouldn't steal a mixer from work, but it was a whisk I was willing to take.

Do you wanna box for your leftovers? No, but I'll wrestle you for them.

I knew a guy who collected candy canes. They were all in mint condition.

My seasickness comes in waves.

"Doctor, you've got to help me. I'm addicted to Twitter." Doctor: "I don't follow you."

A termite walks into a bar and asks, "Is the bar tender here?"

Why aren't dogs good dancers? They have two left feet.

Why do pancakes always win in baseball? They have the best batter.

How do you get straight A's? By using a ruler!

Why was 6 afraid of 7? Because 7, 8, 9!

Did you hear about the claustrophobic astronaut? He wanted a bit more space.

Why are basketball players messy eaters? Because they are always dribbling.

Rest in peace, boiled water. You will be mist.

Why don't pirates take a bath before they walk the plank? They just wash up onshore.

I've been watching a channel on TV that is strictly about origami. Of course, it is paper view.

I was once fired from a canned juice company. Apparently, I couldn't concentrate.

Why couldn't the couple get married at the library? It was all booked up.

What do you call a bear who's into gardening? A Hairy Potter.

My friend said to me: "What rhymes with orange." I said: "No it doesn't"

Why didn't the quarter roll down the hill with the nickel? Because it had more cents.

What's the king of school supplies? The ruler!

What makes the calendar seem so popular? Because it has a lot of dates!

Why is "dark" spelled with a "k" and not a "c"? Because you can't "c" in the dark!

I wouldn't buy anything with Velcro. It's a total rip-off.

My wife told me I had to stop acting like a flamingo. So I had to put my foot down!

What do porcupines say when they kiss? Ouch!

How many months have 28 days? All of them!

What has four wheels and flies? A garbage truck.

What rock group has four men who don't sing? Mount Rushmore.

Where do you learn to make a banana split? Sundae school.

My son is studying to be a surgeon. I just hope he makes the cut.

I was offered a construction job in Egypt. Turned out to be a pyramid scheme.

At the job interview, they asked me, "Where do you see yourself in five years?" I told them, "I think we'll still be using mirrors."

I went to a smoke shop only to discover it had been replaced by an apparel store. Clothes, but no cigar.

What do you call a magician who loses his magic? Ian.

When you have a bladder infection, urine trouble.

A boiled egg is hard to beat.

I used to have a fear of hurdles, but I got over it.

A duck walks into a pharmacy, asks for some lipstick, and says, "Put it on my bill."

Help! There's a letter coming out of the water! It's an emergin' "C"!

It's hard to explain puns to kleptomaniacs because they take everything literally.

5/4ths of people admit they're bad at fractions.

My wife said I should do lunges to stay in shape. That would be a big step forward.

I was excited to hear Apple might start making cars until I learned they wouldn't support windows.

Did you hear about the two thieves who stole a calendar? They each got six months.

What goes through every village, over mountains, crosses rivers and deserts, and yet never moves? A road.

I made a belt out of watches once. It was a waist of time.

Why did the boy throw a stick of butter out the window? Because he wanted to see a butterfly!

What runs around a baseball field but never moves? A fence.

It takes guts to be an organ donor.

I stayed up all night and tried to figure out where the sun was. Then it dawned on me.

The other day, my wife asked me to pass her lipstick, but I accidentally passed her a glue stick. She still isn't talking to me.

Why does Humpty Dumpty love autumn? Because Humpty Dumpty had a great fall.

Did you hear about the campsite that was visited by Bigfoot? It got in tents.

What music frightens balloons? Pop music!

Have you heard about those new corduroy pillows? They're making headlines.

What do you call a dad joke when it gets old? A grandpa joke.

A magician was driving down the street and then turned into a driveway.

A kid decided to burn his house down. The boy's dad watched with tears in his eyes, turned to his wife, and said, "That's arson."

What did one wall say to the other wall? "I'll meet you at the corner."

Why do you never see elephants hiding up in trees? Because they're really good at it.

I'm reading an anti-gravity book. I can't put it down!

What did the ocean say to the beach? Nothing, it just waved.

What did the buffalo say to his little boy when he dropped him off at school? Bison.

I startled my next-door neighbor with my new power tool. I had to calm him down by saying, "Don't worry, this is just a drill!"

What did the plate say to the napkin? "Dinner is on me."

How do you make an octopus laugh? With ten-tickles!

Are monsters good at math? Not unless you count Dracula.

Did you hear about the carrot detective? He got to the root of every case.

I invented a new word today: plagiarism.

Does anybody know where a guy can find a person to hang out with, talk to, and enjoy spending time with? I'm just asking for a friend.

Why does Sherlock Holmes love Mexican restaurants? They give him good case ideas.

What's the difference between Bad Jokes and Dad Jokes? One starts with "B" and the other starts with "D".

Shout-out to my grandma; that's the only way she can hear.

What happens when frogs park illegally? They get toad.

When does a joke become a dad joke? When it becomes apparent.

I, for one, like Roman numerals.

Yesterday, a clown held a door open for me. I thought it was a nice jester.

Why is it a bad idea to iron your four-leaf clover? Because you shouldn't press your luck.

My teachers told me I'd never amount to anything because I procrastinate so much. I told them, "Just you wait!"

Do mascara and lipstick ever argue? Sure, but then they makeup.

Did you hear about the bankrupt poet? He ode everyone.

Why do vampires have no friends? They suck.

Archaeology really is a career in ruins.

My grandfather invented the rearview mirror. Made millions – and he's never looked back since!

To the person who stole my place in line: I'm after you now.

What is the center of gravity? The letter "v"!

Why did the quiz show give away $10,000 plus one banana? They wanted the prize to have appeal.

What do you call corn that joins the army? A kernel.

A slice of mango pie is $2.50 in Jamaica and $3.00 in Puerto Rico. These are the pie rates of the Caribbean.

What is a monster's favorite dessert? I scream.

If a rabbit raced a cabbage, which would win? The cabbage because it's a head.

Spring is here! I got so excited that I wet my plants.

I keep trying to lose weight, but it keeps finding me.

Why is pirating so addictive? They say that once ye lose yer first hand, ye get hooked.

What kind of award did the dentist win? A little plaque!

I asked my date to meet me at the gym, but she never showed up. I guess the two of us aren't going to work out.

My boss told me he was going to fire the person with the worst posture. I have a hunch – it might be me.

The shoe said to the hat, "You go on ahead, and I'll follow on foot."

A man got hit in the head with a can of soda. He's alright though – it was a soft drink.

Which side of the turkey has the most feathers? The outside.

What do you call a boy named Lee who no one talks to? Lonely.

What did Adam say on the 24th of December? It's Christmas, Eve.

I was a bookkeeper for 10 years. The local librarians weren't too happy about it.

What do a tick and the Eiffel Tower have in common? They're both Paris sites.

A cheese factory exploded in France. Da brie is everywhere!

What's a pirate's favorite letter? You'd think it's "R", but it's the "C".

Want to know why nurses like red crayons? Sometimes they have to draw blood.

How do you make the number one disappear? You add a "g" and it's "gone".

What did Tennessee? The same thing as Arkansas.

What was a more useful invention than the first telephone? The second telephone!

Why was the coach yelling at a vending machine? He wanted his quarterback.

Why was the belt sent to jail? For holding up a pair of pants!

Don't trust atoms. They make up everything.

How do celebrities stay cool? They have many fans.

How do you make the number seven even? Take away the "s".

Why couldn't the pony sing in the choir? Because she was a little horse.

Sundays are always a little sad, but the day before is a sadder day.

What kind of music do mummies love? Wrap music.

I used to be a drill operator, but it was boring.

Did you hear about the king who was exactly 12 inches tall? He was a great ruler!

Why did the man fall down the well? Because he couldn't see that well.

Friend: "Bro, can you pass me that pamphlet?" Me: "Brochure."

Some people eat light bulbs. They say it's a nice light snack.

People are usually shocked that I have a Police record. But I love their greatest hits!

What's the longest word in the dictionary? Smiles. There's a mile between the two S's.

If a child refuses to nap, are they guilty of resisting a rest?

What goes up but never comes down? Your age.

"Doctor, doctor, I'm afraid of squirrels!" Doctor: "You must be nuts."

It's not a dad bod, it's a father figure.

What is heavy forward but not backward? Ton!

What do you call a rabbit with lice? Bugs Bunny.

How do you make a lemon drop? Just let it fall.

To the guy who invented zero: Thanks for nothing.

Why was the barber disqualified after winning the race? He took a short cut.

What do you get when you cross a turtle with a porcupine? A slowpoke.

Did you hear the rumor about butter? Well, I'm not going to spread it!

What happens when a snowman throws a tantrum? He has a meltdown.

Ghosts are bad liars because you can see right through them.

What is the difference between ignorance and apathy? I don't know and I don't care.

How do you get a farm girl to like you? A tractor.

I told my kids 10 good dad jokes to see if any of them would make them laugh. But no pun in ten did.

What did the policeman say to his belly button? "You're under a vest!"

Never play leapfrog with a unicorn or a porcupine.

I think my wife is putting glue on my antique weapons collection. She denies it, but I'm sticking to my guns!

Why do standup comedians perform poorly in Hawaii? Because the audience only responds in a low ha.

Why are frogs always so happy? They eat whatever bugs them.

I applied to be a doorman but didn't get the job due to lack of experience. That surprised me; I thought it was an entry-level position.

What do you call a typo on a tombstone? A grave mistake.

I was fired from a job at a calendar factory because I took a couple of days off.

At first, I thought my chiropractor wasn't any good, but now I stand corrected.

What do sprinters eat before a race? Nothing, they fast!

Why didn't the skeleton cross the road? Because he had no guts.

A good steak pun is a rare medium well done.

A horse walks into a bar. The bartender says, "Hey." The horse says, "Sure."

I started a new business building yachts in my attic. The sails are going through the roof!

What do you name an electronic encyclopedia? A facts machine.

What is worse than raining cats and dogs? Hailing taxis!

What do you call a horse that lives next door? Neigh-bor!

Did you hear about the guy who invented Altoids? They say he made a mint!

Wanna hear a joke about paper? Never mind. It's tearable.

Ever heard the rope joke? Skip it.

I won $3 million in the lottery this weekend, so I decided to donate a quarter of it to charity. Now I have $2,999,999.75.

I have a few jokes about retired people, but none of them work.

I quit my job at the coffee shop the other day. It was just the same old grind over and over.

What do you call an alligator wearing a vest? An investigator!

Did you hear about the restaurant on Venus? Great food, no atmosphere.

When I started telling dad jokes like my father, I knew I was full-groan.

Why did the raisin go out with the prune? Because he couldn't find a date.

Why is the letter "A" like a flower? Because a "B" comes after it!

A cheeseburger walks into a bar. The bartender says, "Sorry, we don't serve food here."

Why was it called the Dark Ages? Because of all the knights.

How do you know if a joke is a dad joke? A dad joke has to reach father for a pun.

What has two legs but can't walk? A pair of pants!

What did the toilet-paper roll complain about? "People just keep ripping me off!"

If two vegans get in a fight, is it still considered a beef?

What do Alexander the Great and Winnie the Pooh have in common? Same middle name.

Do you know where you get water from? Well...

There's not much training for garbage collectors. They just pick things up as they go.

I told my doctor I heard buzzing, but he said it was just a bug going around.

How do you get a good price on a sled? You have toboggan.

Show me a piano falling down a mine shaft, and I'll show you A-flat minor.

What word starts with "E" and has only one letter in it? Envelope.

What did the shy pebble wish for? That she was a little boulder.

Why did the pig take a bath? Because the farmer said, "Hogwash!"

What's the best thing about Switzerland? I don't know, but the flag is a big plus.

Shout-out to my fingers. I can count on all of them.

How many paranoids does it take to change a light bulb? Who wants to know?

I used to be addicted to the Hokey-Pokey until I turned myself around.

Where do boats go when they're sick? To the doc.

If the Pilgrims were alive today, what would they be most famous for? Their age.

Did you hear the joke about the pop fly? Forget it. It's way over your head.

What type of horses only go out at night? Nightmares.

What do you call cheese that isn't yours? Nacho cheese.

What kind of roads do ghosts look for? Dead ends!

My first time in an elevator was an uplifting experience. The second time let me down.

Someone complimented my parking today! They left a sweet note on my windshield that said, "Parking fine."

Why did the kid throw his clock out the window? Because he wanted to see time fly!

The world tongue-twister champion just got arrested. I hear they're gonna give him a really tough sentence.

Two guys walked into a bar. The third guy ducked.

Why was 2019 afraid of 2020? Because they had a fight and 2021.

On Thanksgiving Day, why did the turkey cross the table? To get to the other sides.

What did one DNA strand say to the other? "Do these genes make me look fat?"

Granddad always told me things could be worse. He'd say I could fall into a deep hole full of water, but I knew he meant well.

Why can't you hear a pterodactyl go to the bathroom? Because the pee is silent.

Is your refrigerator running? Then you had better go catch it!

I have a joke about procrastination, but I'll tell it later.

A Roman legionnaire walks into a bar, holds up two fingers, and says, "Five beers, please."

How much does it cost a pirate to get his ears pierced? About a buck an ear.

Why didn't the skeleton go to school? His heart wasn't in it.

What did the baker say when she won an award? "It was a piece of cake."

Stop looking for the perfect match; use a lighter.

Why did the can crusher quit his job? Because it was soda pressing.

I thought about going on an all-almond diet. But that's just nuts.

Why didn't the Teddy Bear eat dessert? Because he was stuffed!

What is the tallest building in the world? The library – it's got the most stories.

Don't tell secrets in cornfields.
Too many ears around.

You know what they say about
cliffhangers...

Yesterday I was washing the car
with my son. He said, "Dad,
can't you just use a sponge?"

Why couldn't the lifeguard save
the hippie? He was too far out,
man.

How does a penguin build a
house? Igloos it together.

The first time I purchased
a universal remote control,
I thought, This changes
everything!

What creature is smarter than a talking parrot? A spelling bee.

Why is it a bad idea to insult an octopus? Because it is well-armed.

What do you call a crowd of chess players bragging about their wins in a hotel lobby? Chess nuts boasting in an open foyer.

What do you get when you cross an elephant with a fish? Swimming trunks.

Why is a dad joke like a broken pencil? Because it has no point.

I finally watched that documentary on clocks. It was about time.

Thanks for explaining the word "many" to me; it means a lot.

I ordered a chicken and an egg from Amazon. I'll let you know.

What did one elevator say to the other elevator? I think I'm coming down with something!

Did you hear about the man who fell into an upholstery machine? He's fully recovered.

What do you call a nondescript potato? A common-tater.

What kind of dog does Dracula have? A blood hound.

Why did the crook take a bath before he robbed the bank? He wanted to make a clean getaway!

An angry bird landed on a doorknob. Then it flew off the handle.

The butcher backed into the meat grinder and got a little behind in his work.

I asked the IT guy, "How do you make a motherboard?" He said, "I tell her about my job."

Where should you go in the room if you're feeling cold? The corner – they're usually 90 degrees.

My wife told me to rub the herbs on the meat for better flavor. That's sage advice.

What is the hardest part about skydiving? The ground.

I was going to tell a time-traveling joke, but you didn't like it.

I sold our vacuum cleaner. It was just gathering dust.

What's orange and sounds like a parrot? A carrot.

Why did the toilet paper roll down the hill? Because it wanted to get to the bottom!

How did Darth Vader know what Luke Skywalker got him for his birthday? He felt his presents.

Why is no one friends with Dracula? He's a pain in the neck.

What do you call a factory that makes products that are just average? A satisfactory.

You used to be able to get air for free at gas stations, but now it costs $1. That's inflation for you.

I was fired from the keyboard factory yesterday. I wasn't putting in enough shifts.

What's the difference between a pun and a dad joke? Dad jokes are punnier.

Why did the tomato turn red? It saw the salad dressing.

Why did the house go to the doctor? It was having window panes.

Can a kangaroo jump higher than the Empire State Building? Of course! Buildings can't jump.

My wife and I had an argument about which vowel is the most important. I won.

Someone stole my mood ring yesterday. I still don't know how I feel about that.

What do you call a cow with no legs? Ground beef.

A backward poet writes inverse.

How do flat-earthers travel? On a plane.

What did Venus say to Saturn? "Give me a ring sometime!"

What did one nut say as he chased another? "I'm a cashew!"

Imagine if you walked into a bar and there was a long line of people waiting to take a swing at you. That's the punch line.

Are snails faster without their shells? No, they're more sluggish!

Why is grass so dangerous? Because it's full of blades.

Straws are for suckers.

What type of tree fits in your hand? A palm tree.

I used to work in a shoe recycling shop. It was sole-destroying.

Two clairvoyants meet. One says to the other: "You are fine, but how am I?"

Where do animals go when their tails fall off? To the retail store!

What did the older light bulb say to the younger light bulb? "You're too young to go out tonight."

Why is there a gate around cemeteries? Because people are dying to get in!

Why do porcupines always win the game? They have the most points.

What does a clock do when it's hungry? It goes back four seconds!

How do you measure a snake? In inches – they don't have feet.

I started a new job as a tailor last week. It's been sew-sew.

Dad, can you explain to me what a solar eclipse is? No sun.

I tell dad jokes, but I don't have any kids. I'm a faux pa.

My dad told me a joke about boxing, but I missed the punch line.

If you are going to try cross-country skiing, start with a small country.

What happened when Bluebeard fell overboard in the Red Sea? He got marooned.

What did the judge say when the skunk walked into the courtroom? "Odor in the court!"

Did you hear about the glassblower who accidentally inhaled? He got a pane in his stomach.

Never take advice from electrons; they are always negative.

Why haven't aliens visited our solar system yet? They looked at the reviews...only 1 star!

What does a house wear? Address.

What's the least spoken language in the world? Sign language.

Why do you drive on the parkway but park on the driveway?

Why is the Mississippi River unusual? Because it has four eyes and can't see!

What do you call a multiple-choice dad joke? A pop quiz.

I have a friend who drives a steamroller. He's such a flatterer.

Mountain ranges aren't just funny, they are hill areas.

What did one monocle say to the other? "Let's get together and make a spectacle of ourselves."

What do you call a bear with no ears? A "b".

I used to be able to play piano by ear, but now I have to use my hands.

What state is known for its tiny beverages? Minnesota.

Why is Peter Pan always flying? He neverlands.

Why are fish easy to weigh?
Because they have their own
scales.

How come a man driving a train
got struck by lightning? He was
a good conductor.

What did the finger say to the
thumb? "I'm in glove with you."

Two wrongs do not make a
right, but three rights make a
left.

Why is the obtuse triangle
always so frustrated? Because
it's never right.

Did you hear the one about the
kid who started a business tying
shoelaces on the playground? It
was a knot-for-profit.

Do you want a brief explanation of what an acorn is? In a nutshell, it's an oak tree.

Why didn't the sun go to college? Because it already had a million degrees.

I am terrified of elevators. I'm going to start taking steps to avoid them.

Why do bees have sticky hair? They use a honeycomb.

Someone glued my pack of cards together. I don't know how to deal with it.

What do you call a criminal walking down the stairs? Condescending.

I just found out I'm color-blind. The news came out of the purple!

I was at the library and asked if they have any books on paranoia. The librarian replied, "Yes, they're right behind you."

What did the Zen Buddhist say to the hotdog vendor? "Make me one with everything."

Where did Captain Hook get his hook? From the second-hand store.

How do you define a farmer? Someone who's good in their field.

What washes up on very small beaches? Microwaves.

If a pig loses its voice, does it become disgruntled?

Why was the math book sad? Because it had too many problems.

Past, present, and future walked into a bar... It was tense.

A man dug three holes and said, "Well, well, well..."

More than a century ago, two brothers decided it was possible to fly. And as you can see, they were Wright.

Why are fish so smart? Because they live in schools!

Did you hear about the rancher who had 97 cows in his field? When he rounded them up, he had 100!

Want to hear a joke about a roof? The first one's on the house.

They all laughed when I said I wanted to be a comedian. Well, they're not laughing now!

I asked the surgeon if I could administer my own anesthetic. He said, "Go ahead, knock yourself out!"

What should you do when you see a spaceman? You just park in it, man.

I can tolerate algebra, maybe even a little calculus, but geometry is where I draw the line.

What is tall when it's young but short when it's old? A candle!

A quick shout-out to all the sidewalks out there: Thanks for keeping me off the streets.

How many narcissists does it take to screw in a light bulb? One. The narcissist holds the light bulb while the rest of the world revolves around him.

I ate a clock the other day. It was very time-consuming.

I have a joke about a roof, but it would just go over your head.

Today, my son asked, "Can I have a bookmark?" I burst into tears – eleven years old and he still doesn't know my name is Steve.

Why did the picture go to jail? Because it was framed.

I just got fired from the flower shop. Apparently, I took too many leaves.

Which days are the strongest? Saturday and Sunday. The rest are weekdays.

Whoever invented the knock-knock joke should get a no-bell prize.

What do you call a line of men waiting to get haircuts? A barber-queue.

What do you give a sick lemon? Lemon-aid.

How much does it cost Santa to park his sleigh? Nothing, it's on the house.

Guy told me today he did not know what cloning is. I told him, "That makes two of us!"

I had a dream that I weighed less than a thousandth of a gram. I was like, "0mg."

I had a dream that I was a muffler last night. I woke up exhausted!

How did the hipster burn his mouth? He ate his pizza before it was cool.

How was the snow globe feeling after the storm? A little shaken.

Lance isn't that common a name these days, but in medieval times, they were called lance-a-lot.

What do you call a company started by a group of apes? Monkey business.

They've tried to improve the efficiency of wind farms by playing country music on them, but it's not working because they're really just big heavy-metal fans.

I don't trust stairs. They're always up to something.

Why are toilets so good at poker? They always get a flush.

Within minutes, the detectives knew what the murder weapon was. It was a brief case.

Bigfoot is sometimes confused for Sasquatch – Yeti never complains.

What goes up and down but doesn't move? Stairs.

Young Man: "I've come to ask for your daughter's hand in marriage." Girl's father: "You've got to take all of her or it's no deal."

I have a joke about chemistry, but I don't think it will get a reaction.

Why do seagulls fly over the sea? If they flew over the bay, they'd be called bagels.

My new thesaurus is terrible. In fact, it's so bad, I'd say it's terrible.

Why are mummies scared of vacation? They're afraid to unwind.

What did the 0 say to the 8? "Nice belt."

Why are skeletons so calm? Because nothing gets under their skin.

A skeleton walks into a bar and says, "Hey, bartender, I'll have a beer and a mop."

Why don't sharks eat clowns? Because they taste funny.

What's harder to catch the faster you run? Your breath.

Not sure if you've noticed, but I love bad puns. That's just how eye roll.

Last night, my wife and I watched two movies back-to-back. Luckily, I was the one facing the TV.

What's the difference between a poorly dressed man on a tricycle and a well-dressed man on a bicycle? Attire.

I never wanted to believe that my dad was stealing from his job as a road worker. But when I got home, all the signs were there.

Why did the actor fall through the floorboards? He was going through a stage!

I was just looking at my ceiling. Not sure if it's the best ceiling in the world, but it's definitely up there.

I hate it when people say age is only a number. Age is clearly a word.

Why was the smartphone's camera blurry? It lost its contacts.

What would the Terminator be called in his retirement? The Exterminator.

Why shouldn't you tell an egg a joke? It'll crack up.

Why shouldn't you write with a broken pencil? Because it's pointless.

Can a match box? No, but a tin can!

Did you hear about the mathematician who's afraid of negative numbers? He'll stop at nothing to avoid them!

Why can't a leopard hide? Because he's always spotted.

Did you know that the first French fries weren't cooked in France? They were cooked in Greece.

How are false teeth like stars? They come out at night.

Did you hear about the bread factory burning down? They say the business is toast.

Why did the puppy do so well at school? Because he was the teacher's pet!

What do you call an old snowman? Water.

Why did the stadium get so hot after the game? Because all the fans left.

What type of haircut do bees get? Buzzcuts!

When is a door not a door? When it's ajar.

Why should you never use "beef stew" as a password? It's not stroganoff.

Thanks!

We hope you enjoyed this book.

Visit us at funster.com to discover more books including puzzle books that will exercise your brain while you have fun. It's a relaxing way to spend some quality time!

Email us at: games@funster.com

If you have a moment...

Amazon.com reviews are extremely important and <u>really</u> help us. Could you leave one now? This link will take you to the Amazon.com review page for this book:

<u>funster.com/review30</u>

Browse all Funster books here:
funster.com/books

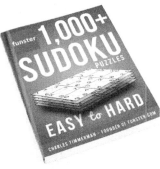

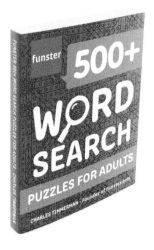

Browse all Funster books here:
funster.com/books

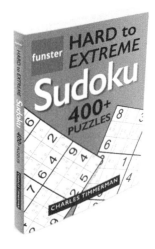

Made in the USA
Coppell, TX
19 December 2022